Seven Keys

to Successful

Single

Parenting

Seven Keys to Successful Single Parenting

From one who has walked the path

SHIRLEY ROBINSON SPRINKLES

Seven Keys to Successful Single Parenting: From one who has walked the path

Copyright © 2011 Shirley Robinson Sprinkles. All rights reserved. No part of this book may be reproduced or retransmitted in any form or by any means without the written permission of the publisher.

Contents

Introduction
What Am I Doing Here Alone?
1

Key 1
Freeze a Positive Picture in Your Mind's Eye
5

Key 2
Hang onto What's Important: Trust
17

Key 3
Put Yourself in Your Child's Place
23

Key 4
Weed Your Garden
27

Key 5

Hang in There! Ride the Waves of Turbulence

31

Key 6

Set Boundaries

37

Key 7

There's Good Information Out There—Ask!

51

Summary

55

Exercises

57

~ Introduction ~

What Am I Doing Here Alone?

Few of us consciously choose to raise children by ourselves. Ideally, we have a partner who shares in the joys and responsibilities of child-rearing—the pleasures and the pains. But life is not perfect; it does not always deal the hand we would choose to play. That said, most of us accept the cards we're dealt and do the best we can to win the game. For myriad reasons, a large number of individuals currently rear children alone. Some have been awarded custody of a single child or, in some cases, a "brood" of children, by order of a divorce court. Others never married or were abandoned by partners who opted out of responsibility. Still others are alone with children due to incarceration of the other parent, or, perhaps, the death. Also, let us not omit that rare single person who bravely steps forward to parent and provide a home for a child through adoption. The range of reasons why you could be here alone is as broad as the Mississippi River. But here you are. Now what?

If you think that a magic genie will appear at this point to provide answers to all of your "now what" questions, let me dispel that notion. After nearly fifty years of being a parent, I can honestly report that "now what" is the most redundantly asked question in life and that it never really gets answered. In many ways, it's like kicking a can down a long, dusty road. As soon as you catch up with it (i.e., think you've got the answer), you must kick it again, and again, and again as you travel toward your destination. The exercise of kicking and the noise the can makes only serve to prolong the entertainment the activity provides. It beats boredom. Eventually, you and the can get to the place you set out for, but not without a few more dents in the can and a lot more dust on the kicker.

The purpose of this book is not to try and answer all of the single parents' or any parent's questions, but to (a) provide some insight into nagging parenting issues commonly experienced by single parents with whom I am acquainted, and (b) to suggest a few divergent patterns of thought and actions that might address those issues in a way that provides ideas that might not have been presented before.

Admittedly, there is no one-size-fits-all solution to be applied to every situation. What are offered here are what I will call "wisdom nuggets" gleaned from my own parenting experiences as a single mother, knowledge learned from reading dozens of excellent books on the subject, and memorable conversations with other similarly situated parents. It was these resources that contributed so much to whatever success I've attained as a mother. Looking back, I realize that it has been a long, dusty journey, and when my end comes, it will have been the single most important journey that I'll ever have made.

When you have finished reading this book, it is my hope that you will feel more confident that you are capable of completing the journey you're on and that you have the right to proudly wear the title of "parent," single, or otherwise.

These seven keys are but a few of the suggestions available to you, but I believe they are essential components of your overall success. Use them to open or unlock doors to the dreams you hold for your family.

Success Components

- Clear Vision
- Strategy
- Practical Systems
- Consistent Applications

~ *Key 1* ~

Freeze a Positive Picture in Your Mind's Eye

Every day, all around us, we see examples of planning made manifest: the car you drive, the clothes you buy, the house you live in, the buildings that make up the skyline of your city or hometown— things that endure and function well are usually products of someone's ideas set into motion. The ability to see things first as images in the mind— as if they were already a reality—is called *vision*. Without it, little would ever get done. Serious visionaries may actually draft a concrete picture of what their finished product should look like. Blueprints, sketches, etchings, and outlines are examples of this.

I'm reminded of a large paper that I keep rolled up under my bed. It is a blueprint of the wooden porch that was added to the back of my house more than ten years ago. At the time, the contractor drew it to give me a clear picture of what I might expect the addition to look like if I were standing in the yard, looking at it from the outside. I could see every feature: the roof, the screened window panels, the decked flooring, the outside deck and steps, and even a portion of the adjacent outdoor area. The paper blueprint is a vivid portrait of what I verbally described to the talented professional with whom I was working. The drawing expressed every detail of the vision I saw in my mind's eye, and it is now my very real, wonderful, wooden back porch. There were no surprises; the contractor delivered what the blueprint promised.

We have all seen examples of such planning and admired the results. Homes designed by architects like Frank Lloyd Wright, Richard Neutra, and Paul Williams might surface in your memory, or perhaps you'll think of your favorite automobile or furniture designer. Parks, monuments, and even recipes are by-products of planning, but this kind of thoughtful reflection should not be confined to the professional world.

How many parents do you suppose devote time to just thinking about what their family will look like before they begin having children? How many do you imagine actually write out a plan? By this, I don't mean color of eyes, texture or length of hair, thickness of noses or lips, height, weight, etc. We tend to think excessively about these physical attributes both before and after birth. Neither am I referring to the career or vocation that we sometimes forecast for our children.

What we most often omit or postpone are plans for the development of character, values, morals, and standards: those intangible traits that make the difference in how our kids turn out, what kind of human beings they will be, and how they will live out their lives in a dynamic and pluralistic society.

Thinking about and planning for this aspect of child-rearing is infinitely more important than any of the aforementioned physical attributes. Why? Because, as quiet as they are kept, these are the essential ingredients of a better world. The future will be shaped by leaders and followers who are today nursing at their mothers' breasts and playing in the play yards of our parks and schools.

"So," you say, "just how do you plan their development?" In a world that seems drunk on vanity, how does a parent struggling to wrest his or her child from the grip of powerful external forces prevail and preserve the sanctity of their parental role in their children's lives? I don't profess to know all of the answers to that question, but here are a few that you might try:

Strategies

> *"You are the architect of your dreams."*
> —Napoleon Hill

A. Develop a long-term vision of family success, person by person.

It takes time and attention to know each of your children as individuals, but nothing is more important to both the child and the parent. No two children are exactly alike, not even twins. Parents help children develop their selfhood. The "who am I" question is best answered by parents. Therefore, to effectively guide and nurture your child(ren), you must realize the importance of getting to know each child as intimately as possible. Not only is this aspect of parenting crucial to positive parent-child interactions, it is also necessary to help you avoid irreversible errors in treating various patterns of your child(ren)'s behavior. Your approach to one might need to be modified when addressing another for the same or similar behavior. As my son, Jonathan, so aptly puts it, "You must become intimate with the problem before you can give birth to the solution."

This notion, called differentiated parenting, may not be accepted in all quarters of society. Many tout the efficacy of treating all of the children the same as a matter of fairness. Stories abound among middle-aged and older adults regarding the "group whuppins'" parents of yesteryear dispensed for the rule infraction of one sibling. Since no one would confess to the wrongdoing that occurred outside of the parents' view, everyone was treated to the punishment. We laugh about those painful episodes now and long for the "good old days."

While these stories are funny to listen to in

the present, careful review of the facts reveals the hostility and resentment that seethed beneath the whimpers of the innocent at the time. Do we want to return to those old, outdated methods? Probably not. It's better to get to know our children and understand them as individuals; this will give us the insight we need to hone in on critical clues given off by our children in regards to individual interests, desires, goals, and unique needs. These are the trails that successful parents pursue as they lead their young ones toward higher and higher horizons of achievements and personal satisfaction. When we know and are aware of our children's talents, personalities, and aspirations, we can then engage them and other family members in establishing the framework for individual success. Together, we can lay the bricks that form both the foundation and the scaffold for successful building.

☙Reflections☙

I wish I had understood this better when I was raising my kids. One of them, my eldest daughter, started telegraphing to me very early that she wanted to march to a beat different from the one I heard in my head. She had a desire to be more than ordinary; she was star-struck in a way that I could not comprehend. She knew the words and the melodies to every pop hit that was spun by DJs on the radio or TV. She was never without a tune, always humming. I paid it no mind. I just prodded her to do her school work and to do her share of the chores around the house. In time, she learned to dance to the music she loved with great agility and expression. I frowned on the time she spent partying with friends, dancing, and enjoying so much social life.

When she became an adult, she followed up on this core interest in music. She took off into the business of producing the records of a couple of talented musical groups. I half-heartedly supported her ambitions, always fearing that she would fail and lose too much money in the process. My fears were realized: she was not successful in that endeavor, but nothing has stopped her in twenty years from loving music. She has found a way, somehow, to stay close to the music industry, these days as an accountant, an occupation she hates but uses to pay the bills. That daughter's destiny is still unfolding. Neither of us knows where she will find the pot of gold she seeks, but I do know that the quest started very early, and I was blind to it. Had I paid attention, who knows where I might have helped her to go?

B. Build a solid nest

If you've ever watched a mother bird prepare her nest, you'll understand what I mean by this admonition. Prior to laying the eggs that will contain the embryos of future offspring, the bird will devote countless hours to the process of finding, sorting, selecting, and collecting just the right assortment of twigs, rags, and other materials to be used in constructing a perfectly sculptured nest. Its walls will be thick, and the nest will usually be placed in a secure location away from the scrutiny of potential animal predators or humans who could harm or destroy the newborns. Have you ever seen father birds helping out with this process? I have. Such wisdom is modeled throughout the natural world of animals. If only we humans would pause long enough to observe its relevance in our own lives!

Single parents are particularly challenged to secure their families from the perils that lurk in freeform throughout modern society. Being ready begins with you. Are you prepared for what you're commissioned to do? A single parent has the daunting challenge of establishing a sense of stability and security for his or her children. Children need to feel "anchored" in order to thrive. When things are tough, keep the vision of a better tomorrow before your family. Keep telling them out loud that things will get better.

C. Keep it real: shoot for the moon, but live in today's reality

It helps to have high and clear expectations early on of how things will turn out, and parents should not keep their dreams and hopes secret unto themselves.

Sharing your dreams of family success builds anticipation and fosters goal-setting among your children. Believe it or not, they want to please you. They long to see you smiling about their accomplishments. That's why active listening is perhaps the most powerful tool of successful parenting. It is better to tell a child you can't wait to go to her first piano concert in Carnegie Hall than to convey the attitude that you don't expect much of her at all.

"Keeping it real" means being real. Our children do not expect us to be storybook or TV moms and dads. They understand that we are normal people, and we do not need to be super people to earn their love and respect. You don't need to be stoic in the face of every situation that confronts you. It's perfectly okay to express feelings of anger, sadness, and disappointment. You are human and should be seen in that light by your children. How you choose to express your feelings makes or breaks the bonds of a good parent-child relationship.

D. Lead by your example

Negative feelings like abandonment and defeat usually follow a separation. It is easy to project blame onto the one or ones that you believe put you in this situation. No matter how tempting, I encourage you to keep naming and blaming out of range of children's hearing. As your child's primary teacher in life, what you do and how you do it will always count as *primo facie* learning. Remember, as author Stephen Covey says, "More is caught than is taught." You, dear parent, are always modeling what is considered approved behavior. Don't be surprised when you get reminded of this when you reprimand a son or daughter for what they've seen or heard you do. "Little elephants have big ears!"

So, how do you express your feelings? Do you throw things when you're angry? Do you curse when you get disappointing news? Do you have fits of crying or whining when you feel oppressed or overwhelmed? Can you identify your patterns of responses to life's challenges?

Along these lines, it's no wonder that so many children have learned to lie to avoid punishment for things they routinely do. Parents lying in front of their children pervades in today's society. Are you guilty, for example, of telling your child to tell an unwelcome caller or visitor that you're "not at home" or "not available right now?" How many times have you promised to either buy them something or take them some place, just to quiet their begging, when you knew you had absolutely no intention of following through on the promise?

Children soon learn to keep score. And what do they learn? They learn that it's okay to lie to get your tail out of a crack. They caught it from you; what else are they catching? Laziness? Slothful habits around the house? Poor eating or personal hygiene habits? How to tell people off through coarse, profane language? By contrast, are they learning essential elements of good communication, like how to dispense kindness and congeniality in dealing with others or how to be truthful and honest in every situation, even when the consequences are not pleasant? Pay attention! You should know what they're learning, at least from you. Your teaching will buffer them from the other things that they will inevitably learn from the outside world.

~ Key 2 ~

Hang onto What's Important: Trust

The very first thing a child learns outside of his or her mother's womb is whom he or she can trust. Trust is a primal need of all humans. First and foremost, a child needs to be able to trust his or her parent. The levels of parent-child trust multiply with time and take on many dimensions. This trust never ends; it extends even beyond the grave. It is an intangible that often takes on tangible characteristics in the same ways as do food, shelter, clothing, financial support, etc. But trust helps confirm feelings of comfort, friendship, love, partnership, and more.

It paints a very sad picture when individuals do not learn to trust. These individuals often develop serious forms of deviancy and exhibit mental health problems, such as schizophrenia, paranoia, and antisocial behavior. That's why it is of inestimable importance that parents establish a solid bond of trust with their children early on. Despite the many other demands of parenting, this trust cannot be overlooked. Trust is foundational to feelings of security and fundamental to the development of high self-esteem. Children of divorce are especially vulnerable in these two areas. Many believe that this is because their feelings of loyalty are severely challenged. The children inevitably hear both sides of the reasons for the breakup, and they feel that they must make a judgment as to who's the most at fault. This is hard for trained judges, let alone children!

Care-giving parents must remain alert to this as their children grow up, and the parents must actively endeavor to keep trust intact between themselves and their offspring. Once lost, trust is virtually irretrievable.

∽Reflections∾

I miscalculated the importance of this principle when I was a young mother. Since I, myself, was a child of divorce, I had never fully developed trust in anyone. Therefore, I took risks with my own children that, knowing what I know now, I probably would have thought better about. Notably, when I was anxious to secure my own release from an unhappy union, I rushed into a new courtship and a new marriage before the children were ready to accept the reality of separation from the only home and father they had known. Although I felt ready for change, my young children were nowhere near ready to shift into a new life with a person who was essentially a stranger to them. The seeds of mistrust were sown then and there, and the turmoil that followed was quite predictable.

One daughter became rebellious and disobedient to a much greater extent than could be considered normal: she lost interest in school, began to skip essential high school courses, and gained heavy interest in the opposite sex far too soon. That path led to dropping out of school and eventually becoming a single mother. She embarked upon a rocky road with seemingly endless bumps.

I caution parents about the temptation to get involved with new people too soon. Inadvertent competition can be set up between you and a new partner that can work subtle havoc in all directions. It pays to wait.

~ *Key 3* ~

Put Yourself in Your Child's Place

A key nugget of wisdom that appears in several self-help books (including the Holy Bible) that has been written by various well-known authors including Stephen Covey states, "Seek first to understand, then to be understood." No other advice exceeds this maxim's wisdom. The way to succeed in relationships—even with your children—is to understand. Understanding evolves from the ability to listen actively. Active listening is a skill that takes time and concentration to acquire; it is not a "given." Do you remember when you wanted so desperately to explain something to your parent, but you were not given the opportunity to tell your side? That's what it feels like to a child who feels that no one really knows or understands him or her because no one ever listens.

When children learn that they will not be heard at home, they find someone else, someplace else, with whom to communicate; there are always others. Many parents discover this too late. Before they know it, their child has formed toxic alliances with individuals whose influences are negative but greater than their own, or after their adolescents have taken on addictions—like abusing drugs, gambling, or sex—that are ruining their lives. You cannot be too busy to hear your child's voice—neither the outer nor the inner voice.

Parents who master the art of active listening hear what is never spoken aloud as well as that which is. They read and understand their children's eyes, body language, and periods of silence. Listening is an art, if not a science. Sometimes the best way to learn it is to observe someone else who seems to know how to do it. Those people are everywhere; look around, and you'll find them.

Key 4

Weed Your Garden

Carefully select your associates. Not everyone is worthy of your time and attention. In a media-centered world that reveres symbols of beauty, sex, fun, and freedom, single parents are challenged to separate the wheat from the chaff among their friends and acquaintances. At times, you may feel that you're missing out on your youth and that life is passing you by. It is normal to be prone to bouts of loneliness and even mild depression from time to time. When this happens, there is a tendency to seek out the company of other adults. Sometimes, just *any* other adult will do. There is no dearth of wandering souls who will gladly fill your lonely hours, usually at the expense of the time and resources you should be spending with your family. I call them "boll weevils"—they're just looking for a home. Stop! Take a deep breath, and consider this:

People who bring alcohol, drugs, foul language, tobacco, or negative or depraved thoughts and actions into your life will eventually, if given the opportunity, affect your children. You need to remain in control of your domain and exclude these influences. It goes right back to the trust element: can your children trust you to protect them from people who mean neither you nor them any good? Think about it!

Domination is another insidious and lethal attribute of some of the people you might meet. This type of personality is found among the most charming of men and women in all stratum of society. It is just as prevalent in churches as it is in bars. I caution you about involvement with individuals who want all of your time and attention and who need to take over all of your affairs, including how to raise your children, under the guise of love. Eventually, you might find the fences of this type of love too confining and smothering. Maintain space for yourself and your children to move about freely in the world.

↦ *Key 5* ↤

Hang in There!
Ride the Waves of Turbulence

If you never experience problems as a parent, you don't live in the same world as the rest of us! Shortly after birth, fantasies of the "perfect child" end. Young children do not learn what "cooperation" means for a very long time, and even after they know its meaning, episodes of cooperation may be very infrequent throughout the growing-up years. If you are experiencing contrary, unyielding tots or teens right about now, you're not the only one; trust me! You're the nanny, but not the one on the TV show! Solutions are not readily available short of murder sometimes (just kidding!), so our hair turns white during sleepless nights while we figure things out day by day, year by year. It's how we earn our Mother's and Father's Day gifts.

Never give up on your child, no matter how trying he or she is of your patience. Keeping your perspective might be hard, but it's your job to stay on the job. Children can take their parents on rollercoaster rides when it comes to behavior. Persistence, positivity, and prayer are the three "p's" that have helped me and others survive the ride. They will help you, too. Parental hugs and kisses are the most effective alternatives to scolding and lecturing. They are excellent for disarming sour, surly attitudes—the likes of which we parents are all too familiar with. Hug and kiss your child(ren) freely and often; when you're gone, this aspect of your parenting may be all they will remember. It will be a wonderful legacy.

⇜Reflections⇝

Each of my children had unique methods of throttling my nerves. My teenage daughter's clothes, tossed wildly about and all over the floor (every floor in the house, to be exact), threatened to drive us all crazy. If not that, then it was the gaudy-looking eye makeup she would put on the second she was out of the door en route to junior high school. Then, there was the youngest daughter's penchant to rebut just about everything. She could argue with a signpost.

My eldest son, on the other hand, said little. He just sucked air between his teeth and made an obnoxious hissing sound that signaled he was not listening and had no intention of doing whatever he had just been told to do. The baby boy, who was too little to engage in such nefarious activities, just sucked his thumb and took it all in, round by round.

Now, they're all grown and have children of their own. I survived and even thrived. It's fun to see what they do now that it is their turn. From where I sit, it looks very familiar. I wonder why?

～ *Key 6* ～

Set Boundaries

I believe in setting boundaries early in the parenting game. Children need to know what they can and cannot do. This is not the same as establishing aspirations, as described earlier; it is about the "rules of the road." While rigid parenting is not recommended, firm parenting is.

The difference is more than semantics: one implies edicts and top-down rules with harsh, non-negotiable consequences, and the other means that standards of behavior are set into rules that are agreed upon by all involved and enforced by parents who honor the value placed on the standards. Appropriate consequences are mutually determined by the parent and the child prior to need and in an atmosphere of trust and collaboration. Application of those consequences lies within the parent's domain, including degrees of severity, flexibility, and duration that he or she may choose. What will happen when a rule is broken should be no surprise to the child, and a parent should not disappoint the child. This is known as "consistent application."

At no time should a child wonder who is ultimately in charge of compliance. Parents should never abdicate their authority in the home. Too many parents today seem fearful of confronting their children regarding their behavior or demeanor. Somewhere along the way, old-fashioned respect has gotten lost in the permissive atmosphere of child-rearing that we now know as the norm. Eye-rolling, door-slamming, and outright cursing gets a "nod and a wink" from parents, teachers, and other adults who deal with children day to day. This occurs because there is limited-to-no adult confrontation. Children and adolescents get away with rude behavior and obnoxious language because adults don't confront them often enough.

Many of us vividly remember the first incident when we "felt our oats" enough to raise our voices to an adult. When we woke up from the daze they inflicted on us with a well-placed backhand slap, we were only too glad to apologize and get on with whatever they had told us to do in the first place. Today, we walk away from the opportunity to confront and teach. I am not suggesting that we take on physical confrontation as our parents were prone to do, not at all. But to say nothing is to give permission. At the minimum, we can establish what's acceptable and what is not. Consider this true story:

☞ Reflections ☞

When one of my sons chose to play all day instead of going to the store around the corner for the carton of milk I asked him to get for me, I deliberately let him do so. Then, when it was dark and time to go to bed, I asked if he had gone to get the milk we needed for breakfast the next day. Sheepishly, he answered no, admitted he had forgotten about it, apologized, and proceeded to get ready for bed. This was the standard operating procedure around our house in those days. This time, much to his surprise, I told him that I was sorry, too, but that the milk was still needed.

"But it's dark outside, and there are bad people on the street now," he said, displaying a pained expression on his ten-year-old baby-face. We lived in Los Angeles, California and he was absolutely right. There were some bad people on the streets, especially after dark.

"I know," I replied. "How I wish you had stopped playing earlier and gone to do what I asked. Now, you'll just have to go in the dark, I suppose." I proceeded to get ready for bed. The look on his face could have caused a storm.

We all went to bed—everyone in the family—but I don't think that child slept much, because at first light, just as dawn was peeking through the clouds, I heard him quietly close the front door, and the squeaking wheels of his bicycle told me he was leaving for the store to accomplish his mission. I will admit that my heart leapt into my throat from sheer, gripping fear! I was probably more scared than he was, but I resisted the temptation to call out to him. Maybe the "bad people" had gone to bed by now. Although only about twenty minutes passed before he returned, it seemed like an eternity! By the time we sat down to breakfast that morning, there was a fresh carton of milk in the refrigerator. I smiled and whispered a very grateful prayer.

This story illustrates a parent's ability to set high expectations and hold a child to them. I had slipped into the habit of taking over and doing my son's chores and other tasks when he failed to perform. It was easier to do them myself than to keep reminding him, I thought. When I realized that he had me figured out, I changed my approach and began putting the responsibility back where it belonged—with him. The more I did this, the more responsible my child became. Today, he is a very responsible man who manages a large staff of personnel to whom he routinely delegates responsibilities, and he expects those responsibilities to be fulfilled. Had I not caught my error, he could have turned out differently.

Responsibility is learned through systematic,

consistent, repetitive routines for which children are held accountable. Tasks don't have to be elaborate. Certainly, they should be within the reasonable capability of the child, but the key is to start early and evolve upward as the child grows to higher mental, physical, and emotional capabilities. Coaching them and then gradually letting them go will be a rewarding experience.

I feel very passionately about this subject. I believe these feelings are rooted in my own upbringing, in which I was taught the value of work. I recently wrote an essay for a publication that I would like to share with you. It expresses quite succinctly why I believe it is important to teach kids to work:

Why Can't Kids Work?
by Dr. Shirley J. Sprinkles

I know that the Feds' intent is to protect children from abuse, but it puzzles me as to why they must go to extremes in some matters. I recently heard a troubling news report about a family that was being brought up on charges because their under-aged children were observed working in the family's pizza parlor. They were reportedly performing simple chores like sweeping the floor, wiping tables, and washing plastic drinking glasses. These activities were not being done during school hours when the children should have been studying formal lessons; it was on a Saturday. The youngest child was about seven years old. "What?" I asked. "What's wrong with kids helping out in the family business?" My larger question is, "How will kids learn to work if they are not taught how and given opportunities to practice?"

When I heard this story, my mind raced backwards in time to the days of my youth when I worked in cotton fields right beside my parents and my grandfather. My job was to attend to the task of picking cotton from the sticky burrs, and filling my burlap–known to me as "croaker"—sack to the brim. The sun was hot out there in those fields, but it was hot for everybody, not just me, as I was frequently reminded when I complained. Learning to endure discomfort was part of my earliest life lessons. I drank cool water from the communal canvas water bag and toiled on—and on, and on, until we reached the end of a long row. "R-e-s-t" took on a special meaning for me as early as five and six years old. Right today I feel that it must be earned.

Kids of my era were expected to do work. We worked at home while our parents were engaged outside the home procuring wages for our daily bread and the roof over our heads. Girls learned to cook, clean, and sew. Some, like me, took on ironing to earn a little cash for ourselves or to help out with the family budget. Boys shined shoes at the bus station, YMCA, barber shops, and on street corners. Some of us even worked in private homes doing odd chores when we became eleven and twelve years of age. There was no *Children's Protective Services Bureaucracy* dedicated to overseeing our private lives and to monitoring whether parents were breaking the law by making us kids engage in constructive use of our time, minds and hands by doing w-o-r-k. Oh, I'm sure there were a few cases here and there of undue, excessive imposition of labor on children. I don't have anything to say that would exonerate people who went to those extremes. But, by and large, work was a positive element in our upbringing—even if, at times, it was hard work.

When I look at many of today's kids, I worry that they will not have the tough inner fiber that was developed in kids from my era. Too many of them don't have a repertoire of skills that complement a balanced adult lifestyle. They are oh-so-technologically "smart," but *survival* "stupid." Girls, for example, don't learn to cook from "scratch" anymore. Who among them can make a flaky, rich pie crust or a flavorful, tender pot roast? Nor do they know how to run an orderly household, or repair a hem in a skirt, let alone darn a hole in the toe of a sock. Boys can't use the tools that my dad taught my brother to use. Screwdrivers, bolts and hinges, plumber's wrenches, planes and saws are foreign to them. Most don't even watch the TV shows that illustrate how these implements are used. Joy sticks and IPODS have replaced the most fundamental hand tools—to the detriment of our kids' basic need to learn to solve everyday problems that they are sure to confront—like the rest of us have confronted and either solved ourselves, or paid someone who knew how to solve for us. I think this is a pathetic state of affairs, and we have brought it on ourselves. Baby-boomers drove the car into the ditch, and now "Gen X" is stuck. What they know how to do is not on the "Help Wanted" list. Schooling, as it exists today, is not doing the job of launching our kids into productive adult lives; the focus is wrong.

So what's a concerned person to do? If schools are going to bypass the practical aspects of one's education in favor of test scores, as they have been doing for a couple of decades, I say that we grandparents owe it to our kids to volunteer in places where we are welcomed to teach the things that make life truly worth living; knowledge of the fundamentals, skills that make one valuable *and* employable in a community, and hobbies that are engaging and enjoyable for a lifetime. We need to go back—way back to retrieve what was lost when w-o-r-k was an honorable four-letter word—even for kids.

☞Reflections☜

To segue to a related, and equally important topic, I'd like to address "allowances" and other means of disbursing money. If your children are like mine, they are very closely attuned to the times when your listening abilities are at lowest ebb. When you're "worn out" from a hard day's work, busy working on the computer, engaged in an intense telephone conversation about business or gabbing with a favorite friend is when they are most prone to need money in an "emergency" way—their version of an emergency, that is. With great acuity and skill, learned from years of observing your behavior patterns, they select just the right moment to catch you off-guard, then hit you up for money to buy that item that they know, under any other circumstance, you would surely deny. It is at times like these when it pays (literally) to stop and listen. You will not be the first parent to be hi-jacked by your own child if you fork over the money in lieu of forfeiting the phone call.

One of my favorite television financial advisors is Suze Orman. I love the way she explains to parents that money should not just be given to kids; that it should be earned by them. I must admit that I was inclined to hand out "allowances" for doing nothing at all except—existing. According to Ms. Orman, this practice of modern-day parents establishes a sense of entitlement that is debilitating to today's kids. According to her, it is not enough to just be born into the world. Children need to feel that they are important, and that they belong to a unit in which they have a functional role in its financial survival. Learning to contribute at a level worthy of monetary reward promotes a type of self-esteem and self-sufficiency that defies description. It is intrinsic and personally fulfilling.

How to handle earned remuneration for contributions made around the home or in the neighborhood is a topic for serious family discussion. Not nearly enough parents, single or otherwise, understand the importance of teaching children early on to save and invest, rather than spending every cent that comes into their possession. The best way to teach this, of course, is to model it yourself. Once again, you must lead by example. Being a single parent does not relieve you of this important obligation. If you can't demonstrate how to save money in a bank account, then do it with a piggy bank—pennies still make dollars—and that's the lesson to be learned.

It is not only in the best interest of your family to embrace the notion of saving and investing, it is also in the best interest of our nation. There are daily news reports that warn of impending financial crises to be thrust upon future generations unless the trajectory of national debt is halted. That "future generation" is your child(ren). That's why there is no compromise to be struck in your responsibility to teach good fiscal practices today, while there's still time. It is said that: "Fortune favors a prepared mind." The wisdom of that saying can be extended to include that fortune also favors a prepared bank account. You and your child must believe in a better future and begin building it right today!

~ *Key 7* ~

There's Good Information Out There—Ask!

Talking with other parents is one of the best ways to find out just how "normal" your child is acting at each stage. Some behaviors are developmental benchmarks. Volumes upon volumes of books in bookstores and libraries describe these stages of growth in great detail. One of my favorites when my children were growing up was one by well-known child psychologist and author, Haim Ginott, called *Between Parent and Child*. (Ginott, Haim G., *Between Parent and Child*, Revised Edition, NY, NY: Three Rivers Press, 2003). Dr. Ginott wrote several books on parenting that are treasured for their humor and timeless wisdom. There were also the famed Erma Bombeck books, (i.e., Bombeck, Erma, *Eat Less Cottage Cheese and More Ice Cream*, Singapore, 1979), and those of Dr. Stephen R. Covey (i.e., Covey, Stephen R., *First Things First*, Fireside, 1994).

Older books like these classics and other more contemporary ones are a good starting point for understanding what may be taking place now and what lies ahead. Responsible parents are "in the know" because they do the research. Those who choose not to read do their learning the hard way: by the seat of their pants. Both they and their pants will quickly wear out. Truly, no book can tell it all. There are some things you'll just have to learn for yourself through trial and error. Experience is still the best teacher. The learning curve can be greatly shortened through reading quality books on parenting and children. You owe it to yourself to seek them out.

~Summary~

So, there you have it. These are the keys, the attitudes, and the Success Components that I believe make a difference between those single parents who succeed and those who do not. There is no magic wand to parenting of any variety—remember that. I do believe, however, that parents have something very special to work from. It isn't a written script, but it is exclusive to parents. I call it instinct. In lieu of an owner's manual, I think we parents get this parental instinct that no one else has, right from the beginning. I say, unequivocally, *trust it!*

We get special feelings when something is wrong with our children. They can be thousands of miles away, and our instincts tell us to call them, just to check out a feeling. Nine out of ten times, we're right. That's what's magical! We also have the instincts to discipline, hug, and kiss our children at the appropriate times and in the appropriate manner if we are adequately tuned in with them. This special gift to us parents comes from the stork, packaged with our little bundle of joy. Instinct tells us when a diaper needs to be changed or when something is wrong with breathing patterns, and it makes us check for fevers or rashes. Likewise, we are able to sense when a troubled teen needs an affirming hug or pat on the back instead of a lecture.

Parental instinct also warns us of malevolent people who are hanging out around our young ones, and it will make us suspicious when a story that has been concocted hastily sounds like a lie. Knowing our children helps activate our natural instincts just when we need them to get to the bottom of trouble. Pay careful attention to them. Use them. Trust them. These instincts can be our best friends. In the Army, there is a well-known slogan that says, "Inspect what you expect." This is very applicable to parenting.

There is no magic that can make our children perfect. Don't waste your time looking for it. Parenting is flat-out hard work. What's more, we get to do it for a lifetime if we're lucky. Despite the truth of this somewhat disturbing thought, few of us, single or not, would ever walk away from the job. There is no more honorable task.

~Exercises~

"What you conceive and believe, you can achieve."
—John Maxwell

The following exercises will give you an opportunity for self-reflection. When we look inside, we sometimes find things that we did not know were there. Make this a personal examination. Use your answers to guide you in either staying on course or re-directing current thoughts and parenting actions. Your success is the goal.

Exercise 1

What words of encouragement have you said to your child in the past 24–36 hours?

Exercise 2

Identify at least one habit or pattern of behaviors that you know you own and display when you are upset?

___

Exercise 3

Who do you know who listens very well? Describe how you feel when you're engaged in conversation with that person.

Exercise 4

What undesirable habit of yours do you think is rubbing off on your child? How is it affecting them?

Exercise 5

What's your story? Have you sown the seeds for mistrust in a child? What was the result?

Exercise 6

Out of loneliness, what tempting relationships have you considered or engaged in that you would not repeat? Why?

_____
_____
_____
_____
_____
_____
_____
_____
_____
_____
_____
_____
_____
_____
_____
_____
_____
_____
_____
_____
_____
_____
_____

Exercise 7

What naughty, annoying, obnoxious, repulsive, or otherwise disagreeable behavior from your child provokes a sense of madness in you? How do you handle it?

Exercise 8

Describe a time when you "just did it yourself" when your child failed to do or to complete a task you had assigned him/her. How often does this happen?

_____
_____
_____
_____
_____
_____
_____
_____
_____
_____
_____
_____
_____
_____
_____
_____
_____
_____
_____
_____
_____
_____

Exercise 9

What is a recent example you have witnessed of a type of disrespectful behavior by a youth? How did you react?

_____
_____
_____
_____
_____
_____
_____
_____
_____
_____
_____
_____
_____
_____
_____
_____
_____
_____
_____
_____
_____

Exercise 10

What are the names of three good articles or books on parenting that you have read this year? With which did you identify or agree? Which ones taught you the most?

∽About the Author∾

Shirley Robinson Sprinkles was born in Greenville, Texas, but she calls Tucson, Arizona her hometown. She attended Tucson schools through the Eleventh Grade; then moved with her family to Los Angeles, California, where she finished high school and college. Shirley graduated from UCLA with a BA in Elementary Education prior to marriage, and ultimately, many years later, achieved a Ph.D in Educational Administration at the University of Texas at Austin.

As she writes this book, Shirley looks back upon a life of peaks and valleys that incorporate the joy and struggles of rearing a family of four children through episodes of marital failures, financial turmoil, and career challenges. She credits her success to the confluence of prayer, family support, persistence, love, and insatiable thirst for knowledge. Shirley is proud of her very successful children and her eight beautiful grandchildren.

Today, Shirley is semi-retired and lives with her husband, Leo Morris, in Austin, Texas. She still actively writes and consults with school districts.

Shirley Sprinkles is also the author of *From Dunbar to Destiny: One Woman's Journey Through Desegregation and Beyond* (Wheatmark, 2008).

www.ingramcontent.com/pod-product-compliance
Lightning Source LLC
Chambersburg PA
CBHW031428290426
44110CB00011B/579

Seven Keys to Successful Single Parenting offers nuggets of wisdom that author Shirley Robinson Sprinkles gained rearing her four children, now all highly successful adults. While this is not intended to be a "how to" book, it is a treatise about complex issues that confronted the author while she was a single parent, issues that may still exist for contemporary single parents.

Although there is no one-size-fits-all approach to parenting, Sprinkles hopes and expects that readers will glean some nuggets of information that will be useful and helpful.

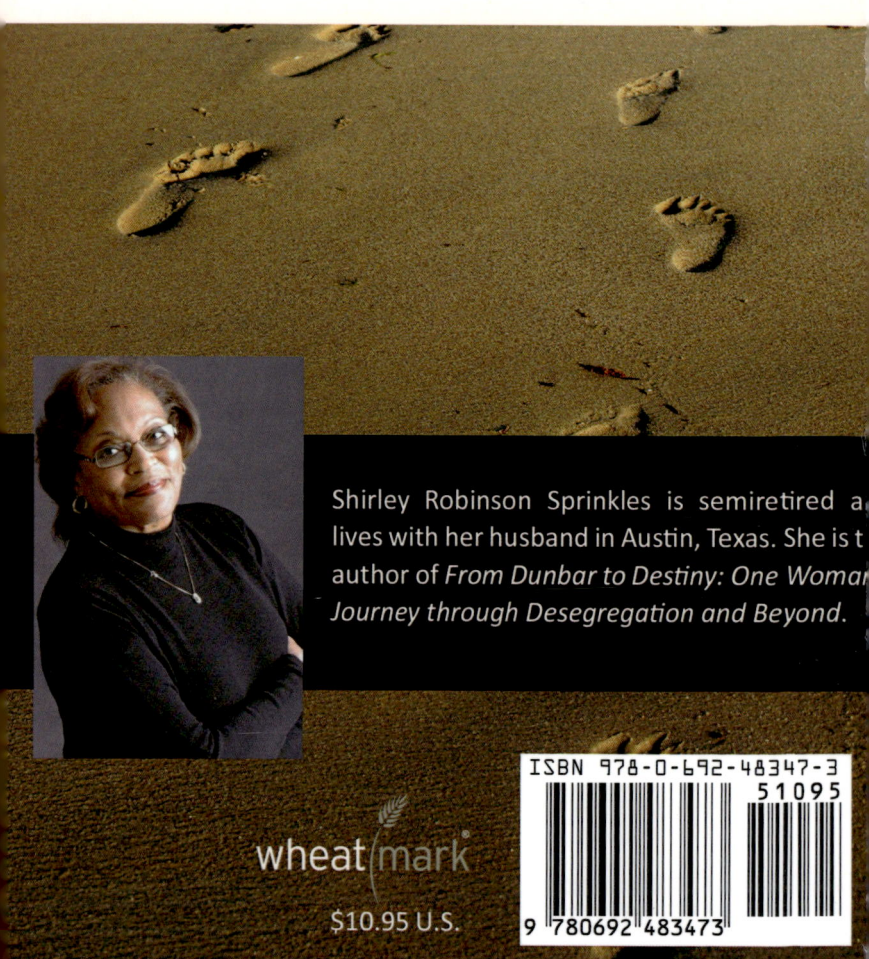

Shirley Robinson Sprinkles is semiretired a lives with her husband in Austin, Texas. She is t author of *From Dunbar to Destiny: One Woma Journey through Desegregation and Beyond*.

wheat/mark

$10.95 U.S.

ISBN 978-0-692-48347-3